SAN FRANCISCO

IN PHOTOGRAPHS

SAN FRANCISCO

IN PHOTOGRAPHS

ERIC J. KOS &
DENNIS EVANOSKY

GRAMERCY BOOKS
NEW YORK

© 2006 Salamander Books
An imprint of Anova Books Company Ltd
151 Freston Road, London, W10 6TH

Published by Gramercy Books,
an imprint of Random House Value Publishing,
a division of Random House, Inc., New York,
by arrangement with Anova Books, London.

Gramercy is a registered trademark and the
colophon is a trademark of Random House, Inc.

Random House
New York • Toronto • London • Sydney • Auckland
www.randomhouse.com

Printed and bound in China

A catalog record for this title is available from the Library
of Congress.

ISBN-10: 0-517-22873-4
ISBN-13: 978-0-517-22873-9

10 9 8 7 6 5 4 3 2 1

Credits

Editor: Martin Howard
Designer: Cara Rogers
Production: Kate Rogers
Reproduction: Anorax Imaging Ltd

Additional captions

Page 1: Haight Street (page 100)
Page 2: California Street Cable Car (page 48)

Dedication

Eric, Dennis and Karl dedicate this book to their sweethearts,
Jessica, Pauline, and Patty.

Acknowledgments

We would like to thank our photographer, Karl Mondon.

Picture Acknowledgments

All photographs © Anova Image Library/Karl Mondon

Contents

Introduction   6

Along the Waterfront   16

North of Market   46

South of Market   74

Heart of the City   90

Outer Neighborhoods   106

Index   126

Map of San Francisco   128

INTRODUCTION

In 1769, Jose Francisco de Ortega, a scout for Don Gaspar de Portola's expedition, saw something other Europeans had failed to notice for over 150 years—San Francisco Bay. Ships had sailed past it since the sixteenth century, but it took a party of Spaniards on land to finally find the body of water on which one of the world's great cities would emerge. Once he got ashore, Portola found that he and his party were not alone. The Alcantara's Yelamu people, one of fifty independent Ohlone tribes, had settled here thousands of years earlier. The Yelamu lived along the shore in areas that later became Crissy Field, Fort Mason, and the Sutro Baths.

In 1775, the Spanish government assigned Lieutenant Juan Manuel de Ayala the task of mapping Portola's discovery. He sailed into the bay aboard the *San Carlos* and dropped anchor near an island he christened Isla de Los Angeles, today's Angel Island. The following year Captain Juan Bautista de Anza arrived from Monterey with soldiers and settlers. Anza looked for a suitable place to lay claim to Portola's discovery, and chose a spot above the headlands for his presidio. He was not the first to find the location attractive; evidence shows that the Yelamu people had lived there over a thousand years earlier. We still remember Anza and his soldiers in

street names like Alviso, Anza, Bernal, Castro, Galindo, Moraga, Peralta, Pico, Sola, and Sanchez. Property rights then served as partial payment for military service, and these soldiers, with their families, originally owned much of the land that makes up today's San Francisco.

A Franciscan priest, Pedro Font, had accompanied Anza and explored the land to the south of the presidio. On the Friday of Sorrows—the Friday before Palm Sunday—he came upon a stream flowing through a canyon. Finding the location suitable for a mission, Font christened the area the Canyon of Sorrows (Arroyo de los Dolores). The Spanish dedicated the presidio on September 17, 1776; the dedication of the Mission San Francisco

Mission San Francisco De Asis: *The birthplace of San Francisco is the smaller building at the left, which has stood on this site since October of 1776. The last surviving mission building, the church is, of course, the oldest building in the city. Mission Dolores Basilica, built next door to accommodate population growth, continues to hold mass in the old mission church today.*

San Francisco Skyline: *The Ferry Building's red lights vie for attention at the center of one of the world's most recognizable skylines. At the right the Transamerica Pyramid and the Bank of America building appear to compete for the title of the tallest building in the skyline. At 853 feet, the Transamerica Pyramid wins by seventy-six feet.*

▲ Ferry Building and the Embarcadero: *This is the view that welcomes those arriving in the city at dusk by boat or ferry. The city's shoreline once ran five blocks further inland along Montgomery Street, but as the city grew, a large seawall was built and a landfill was poured, creating today's Financial District and the Embarcadero.*

de Asis followed three weeks later on October 9. San Francisco was born.

Until 1849, San Francisco remained little more that an isolated outpost, though in 1792 the population did increase slightly when Sir George Vancouver arrived on the British flagship *Discovery*. Though he initially thought that the buildings he sighted were a compound for cattle, Vancouver set up a small settlement, which became a base for European fur traders, explorers, and settlers. Later, in 1822, William Richardson set up a tent store and produced a map that guided ships to anchor in a cove near Vancouver's settlement, rather than in the

1846, when Commodore J.B. Montgomery sailed into San Francisco Bay on board the USS *Portsmouth*. The following day, the United States flag was raised on the square, which took on the name of Montgomery's ship. In 1847, the town's *alcalde* (mayor), Washington Bartlett, renamed Yerba Buena the "Town of San Francisco" and had his new town surveyed by Jasper O'Farrell. That survey shows that San Francisco had seventy-nine buildings, as well as documenting some of San Francisco's first streets: Bartlett, California, Clay, and Howard. Bartlett Street later became Pacific Street and a portion of Howard Street was renamed Sacramento Street.

Perhaps the most important day in San Francisco's history—and certainly the one that signaled the start of its boom from small town to major metropolis—was January 21, 1848. At Coloma, on the American River, 135 miles from Bartlett's newly christened town, James W. Marshall was checking progress on a sawmill he was building. He saw something glistening in the mill's race and went to investigate. What he found changed everything—it was gold. Word of Marshall's discovery spread slowly at first, but on December 5, 1848, President Polk publicly announced the discovery, and the rush was on. By the end of 1849, San Francisco's population had blossomed to 80,000.

The Gold Rush soon led to the establishment of a financial district and an inevitable increase in crime—suspicious fires required the citizens to replace their wooden structures with brick buildings. The city also needed room to grow, so it annexed Pacific Heights and the tract of land now known as Noe Valley. Noe Valley was named after Jose Noe who had served Mexico as Yerba Buena's last *alcalde*, and owned the San Miguel rancho, a 4,000-acre spread in the heart of present-day San Francisco.

Another citizen to leave his mark on the fledgling city was Charles H. Gough, a milkman who sold his product from horseback. As San Francisco grew west of Larkin Street in 1855, Gough was appointed one of three aldermen to lay out streets in the Western Addition. He named one street for himself, another for his sister Octavia, and a third for a friend, a water deliveryman he no doubt saw along his milk route—L. Steiner.

Three years later the Van Ness Ordinance

surf below the presidio. He christened the town "Yerba Buena," for the wild mint that grew there in abundance. At that time a trail connected Mission San Francisco de Asis to Richardson's town and then continued on to the El Camino Real that led to San Jose. This trail became Mission Street.

Progress suffered a blow in 1835 when the presidio garrison moved to Sonoma. Nevertheless Yerba Buena continued to grow slowly. In 1839, an early French settler—J. J. Vioget—mapped the town. His map showed a small square facing the cove. By the mid-1840s Yerba Buena had about fifty buildings, but the town's defining moment came on July 8,

Grant Avenue: *One of San Francisco's oldest streets runs eight blocks through Chinatown, one of San Francisco's most seductive treasures and the home of the largest Chinese population in the United States. Everything the Chinese person (and plenty of others besides) could possibly need or want is available within Chinatown's dozen or so square blocks. The photograph on the facing page shows chickens hanging on hooks in a Chinatown window. Sights like this add to Chinatown's wonderful atmosphere.*

extended the city further westward and allowed for public squares. The author of the ordinance, James Van Ness, had served as mayor in 1856.

On July 4, 1860, Market Street's first horse-car line, the Market Street Railroad Company, began operations. In 1873, Andrew Hallidie introduced the cable car, allowing streetcars to negotiate San Francisco's steep hills for the first time. His first line ran up Clay Street from Portsmouth Square. By 1870, San Francisco's population had reached 150,000, with new housing appearing along the streetcar lines making Downtown more accessible. Hallidie's cable car on California Street also made Nob Hill, one of San Francisco's steepest, accessible as well. Some say the hill's name derives from its shape, others say it is named for the conspicuously wealthy "nabobs" who built their palaces here. Notable inhabitants included railroad magnates Collis P. Huntington, Charles Crocker, Mark Hopkins, and Leland Stanford, as well as James Flood, who made his fortune in silver mines. Today, only the Flood home survives, but the names of three other nabobs live on in hotels atop this prestigious hill: Stanford, Huntington, and Hopkins.

By 1890, San Francisco had grown from a small town with 820 residents, two hotels, and two wharves, to a vibrant city with almost 300,000 inhabitants. But it still hadn't finished growing. In 1906, San Francisco reached Divisadero Street in the west, the bay on the north and east, and Thirtieth Street to the south. Unfortunately for the city's huge population, nature had a shock in store. At 5:12 a.m. on April 18, 1906, the earth shook and everything changed. The Great San Francisco Earthquake and fire destroyed much of the city, and many of its inhabitants found themselves without a home. With typical vigor, though, San Franciscans dusted themselves off, and the city was soon in the midst of a building boom. New constructions shot up

everywhere, including an innovation—apartments now appeared on the landscape for the first time.

Undeterred by the catastrophe, the growth of the city cotninued to gain momentum. In 1918, the longest subway tunnel in the world, the Twin Peaks Tunnel opened cutting the trolley time commute by twenty minutes from Sloat Boulevard to Kearny Street, and making Downtown more accessible to the Sunset District. This allowed further building west of the peaks. Developers stepped in and built Forest Hill, West Portal, St. Francis Wood, and Westwood Park. In 1929, construction began on the O'Shaughnessy Seawall, which was supposed to extend the entire length of Ocean Beach. However, the whole country was plunged into the Great Depression soon after and the poor economic conditions of the 1930s halted construction at Lincoln Avenue.

The Depression and World War II restrained further urban development and San Francisco's skyline remained virtually unchanged until the 1950s when new skyscrapers began to appear. By the late 1960s so many had mushroomed that critics complained about the "Manhattanization" of San Francisco.

At 5:04 p.m. on October 17, 1989, just before the third game of the World Series between the San Francisco Giants and the Oakland Athletics at Candlestick Park, there came a reminder of the terrible forces that lie beneath the city. The Loma Prieta Earthquake struck and seriously damaged the Embarcadero Freeway and the Marina District. There was to be a silver lining though: two years later the city tore the freeway down, breathing new life into San Francisco's historic waterfront. This seemed to spark a new era of restoration and renewal.

In 1993, San Francisco got another reminder of its past. During renovation and expansion of the California Palace of the Legion of Honor, workers discovered a cemetery with 300 bodies from the Gold Rush era. Some were wearing one of San Francisco's most famous products: Levi's. That year also saw a facelift for the South of Market (SOMA) district that includes the Yerba Buena Gardens complex, which also opened in 1993. The nearby Museum of Modern Art opened two years later. In 1998, the city added a newly restored carousel and Mayor Willie Brown took the first ride.

On January 5, 1999, City Hall reopened after a lengthy earthquake retrofit—its golden dome is once again resplendent. The San Francisco Giants began the 2000 season in their new park alongside a far more vibrant waterfront. In 2003, the Ferry Building reopened after a five-year renovation project and on October 9, 2005 the sleek, new De Young museum opened.

Spain's remote outpost has grown into a world-class city that almost 800,000 people call home. It continues to attract millions of visitors each year, many of them unaware that the San Andreas fault might jolt the city into another era of rebuilding and reinvention at any moment.

▶ **City Lights Bookstore:** *A must for booklovers and a unique San Francisco experience, City Lights was founded in 1953 as the nation's first paperback-only bookstore. Two years later, buoyed by its success, the owners started City Lights Publishers with the goal of publishing Beat poets. Today, the shop continues its own legacy of insurgent thinking and anti-authoritarian politics, as is evident from a glance at the shelves.*

◀ **Hyde Street Cable Car:** *Alcatraz and Angel islands provide a breathtaking backdrop to the Hyde Street Cable Car. In 1890, the California Street Cable Railroad opened the O'Farrell, Jones and Hyde line; only the Hyde section remains in operation. The line carries passengers from Powell and Market streets to the Hyde Street Pier, one of San Francisco's most popular attractions.*

▲ **Ocean Beach:** *Luring visitors with spectacular sunsets over the Pacific Ocean, Ocean Beach runs the entire western coast of San Francisco from the Cliff House south to San Mateo County where it opens up into wide expanses of sand.*

Along the Waterfront

Much of San Francisco's charm emanates from its urbanized coastline. This chapter follows the coast north from the southern border of the city then west to the foot of the Golden Gate Bridge.

The eastern coast of San Francisco offered a natural harbor and windbreak to ship captains as early as 1820, and upon the discovery of gold in 1848, the harbor became choked with tall ships from the world over. Many lay abandoned for years, and as the city's population swelled, residents bound the ships together and covered them with earth. As a result, much of today's financial district, well inland, rests upon those buried ships, and San Francisco's waterfront stands at least a mile further out from the original sand dunes on the Bay.

By 1900, the new waterfront had become the most significant port on the West Coast. Local industries boomed, but as outlying communities developed with the arrival of the ferries and railroads, San Francisco took the opportunity to move undesirable operations out of town. The city began to redirect its focus to tourism, with great success—this was its major industry by 1950. Pier 39, Fisherman's Wharf, and the entire bay frontage were transformed from an industrial district for fishermen and longshoremen to a renowned tourist destination over the next few decades.

The Loma Prieta Earthquake of 1989 offered an opportunity to increase the local charm even further when the double-decker Embarcadero Freeway collapsed after thirty-five years of obstructing the water's edge. Today, the city embraces the waterfront once again with an inviting walkway along the Embarcadero offering a view of the skyline and the Bay. One can now walk comfortably from Fisherman's Wharf to AT&T Park where the San Francisco Giants play. Many restaurants line the Embarcadero, and the Ferry Building, renovated to house retail space on the ground floor, offers fine shops and eateries, plus a weekly farmer's market.

▶ **Ferry Building:** *San Francisco's famous landmark received a facelift after being damaged in the Loma Prieta Earthquake. Work began in February 2000 and was completed in 2003. Shoppers and commuters can once again roam the corridors of this venerable San Francisco icon.*

◀ **Monster Park:** *The San Francisco 49ers take the field at Monster Park, which became the new name of the stadium at Candlestick Point in September 2004. The 49ers selected Monster Cable, a San Francisco-based company founded by native San Franciscan Noel Lee, as the team's naming partner.*

◀ **Monster Park, Saint Francis Statue:**

This monumental statue of Saint Francis, the city's namesake, is a gathering point at the stadium. Ground was broken for the park in 1958, and in 1959 the stadium was named Candlestick Park. It officially opened on April 12, 1960, after the San Francisco Giants had played its first two seasons at Seals Stadium. On August 29, 1966, The Beatles played their last concert for paying fans here.

▶ McCovey Cove:
Giant's slugger Willie
McCovey takes a swing in
the cove that bears his
name. Fans have dubbed
home runs hit by Giants that
land on the fly in McCovey
Cove "Splashhits." At last
count there were thirty-nine;
thirty-one off the bat of Barry
Bonds. Only eleven members
of opposing teams have
managed to make a ripple.

◀ AT&T Park: *The
home of the San Francisco
Giants opened in 2000 as
Pac Bell Park. Bought by
Southwestern Bell Corp., it
was renamed SBC Park in
2004. (Following a merger
with AT&T Corp., it reopened
as AT&T Park in March
2006.) The Giants' stadium
features a nine-foot statue of
Willie Mays at the entrance,
as well as an eighty-foot
Coca-Cola bottle with
playground slides and a
miniature AT&T Park behind
left field.*

◀ **"Cupid's Span":** *The Ferry Building makes a backdrop for Claes Oldenburg and Coosje van Bruggen's sixty-foot-high "Cupid's Span" sculpture. The two artists have fashioned over forty large-scale projects for cities, towns, and museums around the world. Architect A. Page Brown used the Cathedral of Seville's Giralda as the model for the Ferry Building's 240-foot clock tower.*

▶ **Union Iron Works:** *Established on the waterfront in the 1850s to build heavy machinery during the Gold Rush, the Union Iron Works were forced to find another market when the gold finally played out. In 1885, it launched the West Coast's first steel ship, becoming known as San Francisco Drydock. It is now a part of SouthWest Marine, which still does repair work at the Iron Works' original location.*

▶ **San Francisco Port:** *Treasure Island's headquarters building and the East Bay hills can be seen in the distance as tugboats lay moored, ready for another day's work at San Francisco's busy port. Maritime activities here include cargo services, overnight passenger cruises, ferry, tug, and harbor services, ship repair, fishing, and fish processing.*

◀ **Embarcadero:**
The Loma Prieta earthquake
severely damaged the
Embarcadero Freeway,
which had long divided
the waterfront and the
Ferry Building from
Downtown. When the
freeway was torn down in
1991, a grand palm-lined
boulevard was created,
squares and plazas
appeared, and the Muni
extended the N and F lines
to run along the
Embarcadero.

▲ **Gandhi Statue:** In
1988, the Gandhi Memorial
International Foundation
presented this life-sized,
bronze statue of Mahatma
Gandhi to San Francisco. It
is not unusual to see the
proponent of peace
garlanded with fresh flowers,
and the statue has become
one of the city's landmarks.
Friends and dates arrange to
meet here and vendors at
the Ferry Building farmer's
market advertise "our stand
is near the Gandhi statue."

▲ **Fog City Diner:**
"Get in Here" the sign in the
diner's doorway demands,
and those who obey will not
be disappointed. Inside is one
of San Francisco's most
recognizable restaurants.

Favorites on its menu include
exquisite spicy sirloin chili,
triple clam chowder, and
red curry mussel stew. Diners
can also take in a panoramic
view of the palm-lined
Embarcadero.

Pier 39: *With more than 110 stores, thirteen full-service restaurants (all with Bay views), and numerous fun-filled attractions, Pier 39's two-level design complements one of San Francisco's most unique retail districts. A feast for the serious shopper, everything from NFL merchandise to jewelry and imported chocolates can be found here.*

Pier 39, Sea Lions: *K Dock on Pier 39 Marina is the home of the much-loved California sea lions. These playful pinnipeds entertain millions of visitors each year and can be viewed close up. And they don't charge a dime! Volunteers and staff at the Marine Mammal Store and Interpretive Center constantly monitor the sea lion population and provide information to guests from all over the world.*

▲ **Alioto's:** *Some say the true flavor of San Francisco is found in its seafood, fresh from the ocean and perfectly prepared. Alioto's has been serving Sicilian delicacies, homemade pastas, seafood risotto, seafood sausage, and shellfish cioppino since 1925. The restaurant's three-tiered dining room offers every guest stunning views of San Francisco Bay.*

▶ **Fisherman's Wharf:** *Fishing boats stand ready to brave the elements at this famous wharf. Among the fleet are grandsons and great-grandsons of yesterday's fishermen, still operating family-owned boats. Fisherman's Wharf is a bustling place, a working wharf that has managed to preserve its traditions.*

◄ **Wax Museum:** *The architecture of San Francisco's Wax Museum was inspired by the city's traditional building designs. It features spectacular domes, ornate bay windows, ornamental metalwork, and complex rooflines. The artistic use of brick, stucco, metal, and glass lend a fresh, new appeal to the much beloved unique San Francisco style.*

▲ **Wax Museum, Interior:** *Lance Armstrong and Barry Bonds do their thing at the Wax Museum. They join a galaxy of stars that includes Leonardo DiCaprio, Will Smith, Humphrey Bogart, Marilyn Monroe, and John Wayne. The World Leaders section is presided over by the American president while the Hall of Religion is populated with the figures of many august men and women, including the current pope.*

◀ **Musée Mécanique, Laughing Sal:** *Sal delivers her infectious cackle just inside the door of the museum, where an animated six-foot mannequin in Gold Rush attire serves as the museum's greeter. The job is nothing new to Sal; she's been greeting folks in San Francisco since the early 1930s, and once had the same gig at Whitney's Playland at the beach. Visitors can also stop by and say hello to her colleague, Naughty Marietta.*

▲ **Musée Mécanique:** *San Francisco's beloved Musée Mécanique survived its eviction from the Cliff House and in August 2004 reopened at Fisherman's Wharf. Admission is free, but visitors are well advised to bring a pocketful of quarters to animate the museum's many fascinating gadgets and machines.*

▶ **USS *Pampanito:*** *The troop ship Jeremiah O'Brien dwarfs the submarine USS Pampanito at Fisherman's Wharf. A National Historic Landmark, the Pampanito hosts approximately 110,000 visitors a year and is one of the most popular historic vessels in the country. The Jeremiah O'Brien is the only still-active survivor of the great D-Day armada.*

◁ **Ghirardelli Square:**
"Say Gear-ar-del-i" the advertisements once coaxed chocolate lovers. Over a century ago, Ghirardelli Square was home to the family's chocolate, cocoa, mustard, and box factory after the company relocated here in 1895. The city of Sausalito nestled on a hill across the bay and Mount Tamalpais help complete a memorable picture for passengers arriving aboard cruise ships.

▷ **Ghirardelli Square:**
The square was declared an official city landmark in 1965 and has been granted National Historic Register status. Visitors might also remember the location from the movies: Clint Eastwood once roamed the square in Dirty Harry.

◁ **Ghirardelli Square:**
Picturesque Ghirardelli Square makes a perfect place to end a busy day along the San Francisco waterfront. Today, the square features remarkable restaurants, galleries, and specialty shops, as well as breathtaking Bay views and beautifully landscaped plazas.

◀ **Baclutha:** *Shipping in San Francisco has a long history and is still very much a part of the city's culture. The Baclutha, seen here in the foreground, exhibits that maritime legacy while a state-of-the-art cruise liner passes by. Baclutha, once the Star of Alaska, a member of the Alaska Packers fleet, sailed the waters of Alaska, bringing salmon back to her berth in Alameda across the San Francisco Bay.*

▲ **San Francisco Ferries:** *Before the advent of the automobile, most Bay Area residents commuted using railroads and ferries; around 1930, the Ferry Building saw 250,000 people per day pass through its doors. Today, high speed ferries like these are making a comeback, carrying passengers under the shadow of striking landmarks such as Alcatraz and the 2,751-foot Mount Tamalpais.*

◀ **Golden Gate Bridge:** *Spanning the entrance to San Francisco Bay, the Golden Gate Bridge is the most recognizable landmark in the city. Completed in 1937, ahead of schedule and under budget at thirty-five million dollars, this marvel of engineering spans 4,200 feet. Engineer Joseph Baerman Strauss defied critics who said the bridge could not be built.*

▲ **Fort Point:** *Artillery improvements that rendered third-system brick forts useless meant that Fort Point was already obsolete on its completion in 1861. By the turn of the century, the U.S. Army was using it only for storage. However, Golden Gate Bridge engineer Joseph Strauss found a use for the fort and made it the base of his construction operations. No shot has ever been fired from Fort Point.*

▶ **San Francisco-Oakland Bay Bridge:** *This magnificent engineering feat is the longest steel high-level bridge in the world, with the tallest bore in the world passing through Yerba Buena Island. Opened in 1936, the bridge required more funding than almost any other single structure in history, but still took only three years and four months to complete. The Bay Bridge spans eight and a quarter miles and uses 70,815 miles of cable— enough to circle the earth three times. Today more than 275,000 vehicles cross the bridge daily.*

Crissy Field: *Originally a rich salt marsh and gathering ground for native people, Crissy Field was later the landing site of explorers and traders. In 1915, the Panama Pacific International Exposition was held here, and shortly after the area became one of the country's most important military airfields. Today, Crissy Field is spectacular national parkland.*

◀ **Palace of Fine Arts:**
The sun rises over architect
Bernard Maybeck's Palace of
Fine Arts. Maybeck designed
the building for the 1915
Panama Pacific Exhibition,
after which San Franciscans
saved it from its planned
demolition. More than ninety
years later, it is still a tourist
attraction. The Exploratorium,
a collage of science, art, and
human perception exhibits, is
housed within its walls.

▲ **St. Francis Yacht**
Club: The club was founded
in 1927 on the site of Stone's
Boat Yard and hosts over
forty regattas on San
Francisco Bay each year,
including the annual Big Boat
Series every September. It
was also the location of the
2000 U.S. Olympic sailing
trials. Today, it caters to the
interests of its 2,300-plus
members, which include
racing, cruising, sailboarding,
kiteboarding, water-skiing, and
more. Club members have
both challenged for and
defended the America's Cup,
and also brought home
Olympic medals.

North of Market

This chapter visits the many neighborhoods just a few blocks inland from the water, north of Market Street and east of the Presidio.

A landmark visible from far and wide, Coit Tower stands atop Telegraph Hill in the northeast corner of the city and commemorates fallen firefighters from the city's past. The views from the tower are unrivalled. Just further southwest, two ethnic neighborhoods, North Beach and Chinatown, are two of San Francisco's crown jewels. San Francisco's Little Italy, North Beach, seamlessly combines favorite Italian restaurants and a Catholic cathedral with music venues, historic strip clubs, and the City Lights Bookstore, a favorite haunt of Jack Kerouac and the Beat poets. Chinatown gives tourists and townies alike a chance to step outside the United States for a moment. The local, predominantly Chinese, population caters to millions of visitors who flood Grant Street each year. Just around the corner,

another Chinatown maintains a deep cultural resemblance to China itself and ignores the tourists.

The skyscrapers that form the city's famous skyline stand in the Financial District and Downtown, humming with commerce on weekdays. Pacific Heights, just up the hill, houses some of San Francisco's wealthiest residents as well as Grace Cathedral. Russian Hill got its name from the population that originally settled there, and is perhaps best known for Lombard Street, the quintessential San Francisco landmark, which winds its way down the back of the hill.

In the days of Mexican California, an unpaved road connected the military settlement at the Presidio with Mission Dolores and the small pueblo. Along the road several dairy farmers raised cattle and the area's nickname, "Cow Hollow," stuck. Today Union Street, one of San Francisco's busier shopping boulevards, follows the path of that unpaved road.

▶ **Huntington Hotel and Nob Hill Spa:** *Built in 1924, the hotel and spa recalls Collis P. Huntington, one of Nob Hill's nabobs. The site of his magnificent mansion, which was destroyed by the 1906 earthquake and fire, was donated to the city by the magnate's family and is now Huntington Park.*

◄ **California Street Cable Car:** *A San Francisco icon, the cable car here rolls its way down California Street with the Bay Bridge in the distance. Andrew Smith Hallidie got the idea for the cable car after seeing a horse-drawn carriage slide backwards down a San Francisco hill on a damp summer day. He tested his first one in August 1873.*

▲ **Cable Car Museum:** *Within the historic Cable Car Barn and Powerhouse, visitors can view the actual machinery responsible for propelling the city's cable cars. The cables run on a pulley system, which the cars themselves attach to, and then are dragged through town. The gears seen here are pulling cables.*

◄▲ Coit Tower: *The funds to build San Francisco's 210-foot-tall Art Deco icon were donated by Lillie Hitchcock Coit. The unpainted, reinforced concrete tower was dedicated in 1933. Coit tower stands atop Telegraph Hill, where observers once went to identify ships coming through the Golden Gate. They used mechanical signals called "telegraphy" to relay this information to interested parties, such as financiers, merchants, wholesalers, and speculators.*

▶ **Coit Tower,
Interior:** *Inside, the tower
is filled with art, depicting
agriculture, education, urban
and rural life, and social
protest. Here Mallette Harold
Dean's "Stockbroker" looks on
as workers in Maxine Albro's
mural reap the riches of
California's soil. The
"Stockbroker" is said to be a
likeness of Bank of America
founder A.P. Giannini's son,
Steve. The project was funded
by the Works Progress
Administration's Federal
Art Project.*

◄ **Barbary Coast:**
This historic part of the city grew from Sydney Town, the area at the foot of Broadway and Pacific Street, and once catered to miners who had spent months in the wilderness. Hungry for female companionship and bawdy entertainment, they flocked to the dance houses and concert saloons here, some of which still survive. Big Al's, the Condor, and the Hungry I are three famous examples.

▲ **Dick Hotaling's Whiskey Warehouse:**
Located on Jackson Street, the warehouse is notable for not burning to the ground during the devastating fire that followed the 1906 earthquake. At the time its lucky escape inspired a ribald poem that asked, "If God spanked the town for being over-frisky, why did he burn the churches down and spare Hotaling's whiskey?"

▷ **Saints Peter and Paul Church:** *The church was originally located at Filbert Street and Grant Avenue until the 1906 earthquake razed it to the ground. Its Neo-Gothic replacement was built in 1924 and now serves the North Beach Roman Catholic community. The photograph shows the church's 191-foot-tall twin spires against the homes that dot Telegraph Hill.*

◀ **Bimbo's 365:** When the two first met, Monk Young was unable to pronounce Agostino Giuntoli's name and instead dubbed him "Bimbo," the Italian word for "boy." In 1931, the pair opened the 365 Club at 365 Market Street and twenty years later Bimbo's moved to Columbus Street. With its red-curtained walls, sparkly chandeliers, and tuxedo-clad bartenders, Bimbo's 365 is a great place to relive the good old days.

▲ **Broadway and Columbus Mural:**

Designed in 1987 by Bill Weber and Tony Klaas, this mural at the intersection of Broadway and Columbus represents the history of North Beach and Chinatown. Depicted are such icons as Emperor Norton, jazz musicians, Italian fishermen, the Imperial Dragon, and Herb Caen. Benny Goodman plays clarinet and Oscar Peterson, bass.

▶ **The Stinking Rose:**

At last count, 2,635 bulbs of garlic, two onions, and one leek festooned the nooks and crannies of The Stinking Rose: A Garlic Restaurant, which serves 3,000 pounds of the pungent herb monthly. The restaurant offers full-on garlic fare for the truly adventurous, mild for the novice, and "sans" garlic for those finding the herb's folklore and aroma more appealing than its taste.

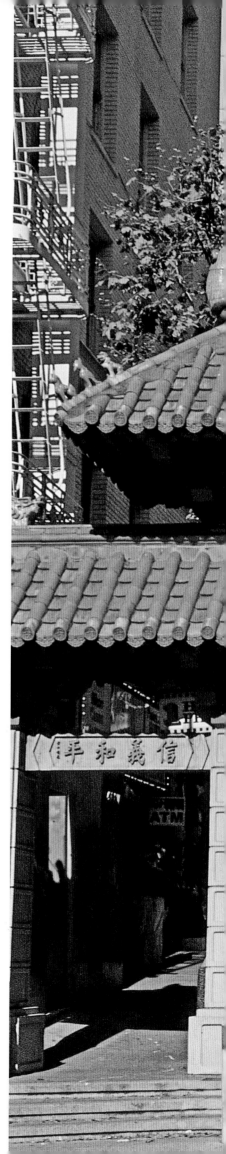

▲ **Hang Ah Restaurant:** *This is the oldest Dim Sum restaurant in San Francisco and is frequently given rave reviews as one of the best Chinese restaurants in a city that's full of great Chinese food. Dim sum are the savory snacks popular for brunch in parts of China and include pork buns, deep-fried curried-beef rolls, translucent steamed shrimp dumplings, and pot stickers.*

▶ **Chinatown Gate:** *Built in 1970 at Bush Street and Grant Avenue, the gate marks the transition from Union Square to Chinatown. Beyond are the Dragon Lights—ornate streetlights added in 1925. Today's Chinatown arose from the ashes of the 1906 earthquake; its architecture a mix of Edwardian fundamentals and Chinese details.*

The Goddess of Democracy: *Supporters of democracy raised the original statue in Beijing's Tiananmen Square, China, during the June 1989 uprising. This replica stands in Portsmouth Square and was a gift from the San Francisco Goddess of Democracy Project and artist Thomas Marsh to the City and County of San Francisco.*

Tadich Grill: *In one form or other, the Tadich Grill has been around since 1849. It began as a simple coffee stand, then became the New World Coffee Saloon, and later the Cold Day Restaurant. Eventual owner John Tadich arrived from Croatia in 1871, and in 1928 he renamed the place "Tadich Grill, The Original Cold Day Restaurant."*

◀ **Sentinel Building:**
With its copper-clad facade,
aged to a pastel green, the
Sentinel Building at Third and
Market Streets exemplifies
"flatiron" construction in San
Francisco. Over the years the
elegant building has seen
many famous and infamous
people walk through its
doors. Notorious political boss
Abe Ruef once had offices on
the top floor, while "Caesar's,"
the company credited with
creating the salad of the
same name, was also located
here. Film director Francis
Ford Coppola bought and
restored the building in the
early 1970s, and it is now
home to his American
Zoetrope Studios.

▶ **Sentinel Building,**
Entrance: William
Randolph Hearst once ran
his San Francisco Examiner
empire from the Sentinel
Building, and in 1937 hired
renowned architect Julia
Morgan to restore it to its
pre-earthquake glory. She
added a marble lobby and
decorated the facade to
make an impressive entrance
with a cartouche of the letter
"H" in tribute to her client.

◀ **Geary Theater:**

Designed in 1908 by architects D. Bliss and William B. Faville—whose portfolio includes the St. Francis Hotel—the theater went through several name changes before finally becoming the Geary Theater in 1928. For the next forty years, the major players of the American stage performed here. In January 1967, the Geary Theater became the home of the American Conservatory Theater.

▶ **Lotta's Fountain:**

Lotta Crabtree, one of the city's most popular entertainers, gave this fountain to San Francisco in 1875. After the 1906 earthquake, it became a gathering point for survivors and names of the dead, the missing, and the found were posted here. Every year since, on April 18, at 5:13 a.m., living survivors gather. (In 2005 the oldest was 104.) Although the number of this unique group diminishes each year, the early morning tribute still draws crowds.

John's Grill: *This historic restaurant is one of the city's oldest and most famous establishments, as well as an established literary landmark. It was made famous by Dashiell Hammett's 1930 mystery novel,* The Maltese Falcon, *and later the movie of the same name starring Humphrey Bogart. That legacy is today celebrated on the grill's menu. The "Sam Spade Lamb Chops" are particularly good.*

Flood Building: *James C. Flood was one of the owners of the Consolidated Virginia Mine and its "Big Bonanza." Such was his wealth that he and his associates, John Mackay, James Fair, and William O'Brien became known as the Bonanza Kings. In 1902, he purchased the land that held the remains of the Baldwin Hotel and hired architect Albert Pissis to erect a building to honor his late father James Clair Flood. The twelve-story, 293,837-square-foot building cost $1,500,000 and was the largest building in the city of San Francisco at*

◀ **California Street Cable Car:** *Cable cars on this famous route are drawn on steel cables, which range in length from 10,000 feet to over 21,000 feet. A 500 horsepower DC electric motor keeps each cable car moving at exactly 9.5 miles per hour. This car passes Grace Cathedral on its way Downtown.*

▲ **Grace Cathedral:** *This is the replacement of the historic Grace Church, which was destroyed in the 1906 earthquake. The cathedral was built on land donated by the Crocker family. The magnificent building is famed for its Ghiberti doors, the Gates of Paradise, labyrinths, varied stained glass, medieval and contemporary furnishings, as well as its carillon, organs, and choir.*

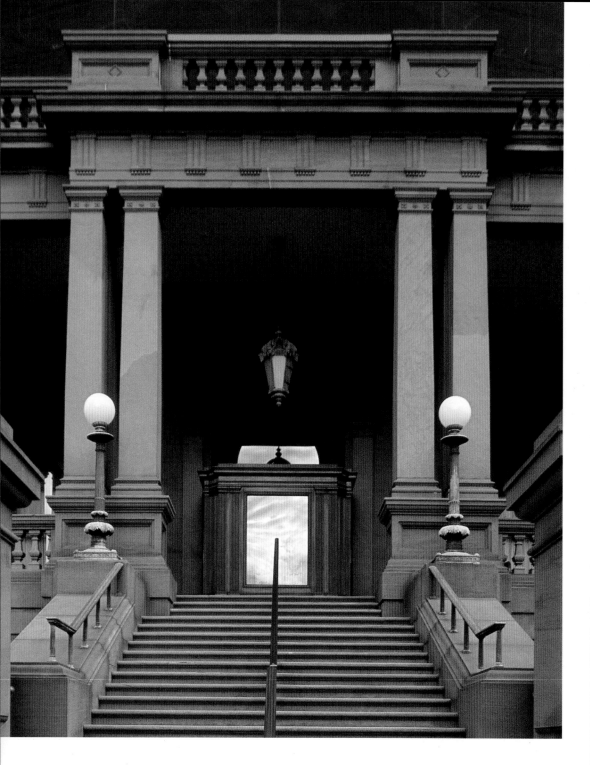

▲ **Flood Mansion:**
Bonanza King James Flood built his Nob Hill mansion of Connecticut brownstone and hired the W. T. Garratt foundry to surround it with the most expensive bronze fence in the city. Flood even went so far as to hire someone to keep it polished. The home survives today as the Pacific Union Club. After the interior burned in 1906, it was redesigned by Willis Polk, who also added wings and a third floor.

▶ **Fairmont Hotel:** *The brainchild of Bonanza King James Fair's daughter Tessie Fair Oelrichs, the Fairmont Hotel was originally built in 1906. It was on the verge of opening its opulent doors when the earthquake struck and wrecked the building. Despite the setback, architect Julia Morgan was hired to restore and complete the building, which opened to the public exactly one year later.*

◀ **Haas-Lilienthal House:** *Peter Schmidt designed this Queen Anne-style house on Franklin Street for grocer William Haas and his family in 1886. Built entirely of redwood, the building boasts authentic furniture and artifacts, elaborate wooden gables, a circular corner tower, and luxurious ornamentation. Although it might appear opulent today, the 11,500-square-foot house was considered a standard San Francisco middle-class home when Haas purchased the land for $13,500 and built the house for $17,500.*

▶ **Lombard Street:** *The Hyde Street Cable Car crosses the crest of Lombard Street, generally known as San Francisco's crookedest street. The eight sharp bends were introduced during re-engineering work in 1922 to help motorists deal with the twenty-seven-degree slope. According to* Ripley's Believe It Or Not, *Lombard Street is not the crookedest street in the world, and others say Lombard Street is not even the most crooked street in San Francisco—Vermont Street on Potrero Hill disputes the claim.*

South of Market

Market Street serves as the principal boulevard of the city, running through many significant parts of San Francisco. South of Market boasted a booming industry in years past, but has undergone a cultural renaissance; several recently added and other perennial San Francisco landmarks reside here. Yerba Buena Gardens, an urban park, adjoins the San Francisco Museum of Modern Art and the Metreon, a mall and movie theater. Also nearby are the Moscone Convention Center and the Old U.S. Mint.

Down Mission Street, one discovers the Mission, a primarily Latino neighborhood. This has long been a Mexican settlement and is even older than San Francisco itself. It was here that the pueblo of Yerba Buena stood next to a small lagoon of the Bay, and Mission Dolores served as the first church. Founded in 1776, Mission Dolores still stands.

Further west, the Castro, the self-proclaimed "Gay Capital of the World," reinforces San Francisco's reputation for accepting all people. Bernal Heights got its name from the original 1939 Mexican grantee, Jose Cornelio de Bernal. Bernal's land was subdivided in 1860 and has been inhabited by some shady characters at various times. Conmen once planted traces of gold in the heights, sparking a mini gold rush around 1870. Since the 1980s, Bernal Heights has gentrified. Nearby Potrero Hill (potrero meaning pasture in Spanish), fed many Mission Dolores cattle until industry brought in sugar, steel, and canning businesses during the twentieth century. Some still operate in the area, but a residential neighborhood also thrives today. As we travel further south and west, the neighborhoods become residential retreats clinging to the hillsides. Noe Valley offers Victorian living in famous old rowhouses as well as convenient shopping, while Twin Peaks gives residents on the slopes some striking views of urban San Francisco, just a short ride away.

▶ **Metreon:** *This complex is the largest movie house in the city and was built in the 1990s along with the adjoining Yerba Buena Gardens. Offering sixteen theaters, including an Imax theater reputed to contain the largest 3D screen in the world and an arcade featuring the latest digital games, the Metreon is the place to find new visual technologies.*

▲ **Market Street:**
Market Street, the city's main ceremonial and commercial boulevard, runs from the Ferry Building on the Bay, through the center of town near City Hall, and southwestward. The first and most significant center of transit—and therefore commerce—Market Street had streetcars as early as 1860, as well as some of the best shopping in town.

▶ **San Francisco Museum of Modern Art:** Originally founded in 1935 and the first West Coast museum to exclusively display twentieth-century art. The word "modern" was added to the museum's name in 1975. In 1995, the SFMOMA opened a new building, designed by Swiss Architect Mario Botta, in the rapidly redeveloping South of Market area.

Streetcars: *Different from cable cars in that they are powered by electricity, these cars travel Market Street and the Embarcadero. Transit advocates moved to have streetcars reinstated in 1971, but the project did not get underway until the Embarcadero Freeway came down after 1989. Today, the streetcars again make up a part of the city's unique personality.*

◀ **Old United States Mint:** *Completed as San Francisco's second mint by 1874, this granite building was untouched by the Great San Francisco Earthquake and Fire, and helped provide redevelopment capital after the disaster. It closed in 1937 but was restored in 1976. City officials suggested reusing the building as the home of the San Francisco Museum in 2003.*

▲ **Cartoon Art Museum:** *Cartoon art enthusiasts founded this unique museum at 665 Mission Street in 1984, at first exhibiting personal collections in an open-air gallery. With a donation from Peanuts creator, Charles M. Schulz—a Bay Area native— the museum later found a permanent home in Yerba Buena Garden's art center. The museum has produced almost ninety exhibits and twenty publications since its inception.*

◀ **Mission Street:**
The main boulevard of the
Mission District provides
visitors with many of the
same types of businesses
found in Latin America.
Taquerias, pupuserias, and
Salvadorian bakeries show
how the Latin side of San
Francisco blends with the
cafés, thrift shops, and
alternative-style American
shops.

▶ **The Mission
District:** A neighborhood
which took its name from
nearby Mission Dolores and
is populated largely by
Mexican and Central
Americans. This area also
attracts offbeat artists who
have decorated many blank
walls with murals celebrating
Hispanic heritage and human
rights. Known as the city's
first neighborhood, the
Mission often doesn't make
the tourist circuit and has
always offered affordable
living for the young and the
artistic.

◀ **Mission San
Francisco de Asis:**
Many of the original stones
from mission-era burials are
still to be found in the resting
place of the first mayor of San
Francisco, Don Francisco de
Haro. San Francisco de Asis is
the official Spanish name for
this mission, but the site is
also known as Mission
Dolores for the adjacent (now
dry) Laguna de los Dolores
(Lake of Our Lady of Sorrows).

◀ **Dolores Park:** Clear views of the Downtown skyline are visible from Dolores Park, established in 1905. A year after it opened, the park served as a refugee camp for 1,600 families made homeless by the Great Earthquake and Fire.

▲ **Castro:** The self-proclaimed "Gay Capital of the World," the Castro neighborhood took its name from Castro Street. The 1978 assassination of openly gay city supervisor Harvey Milk caused its residents to proudly proclaim their sexuality in the face of adversity. Today, annual events such as the Castro Street Fair and the famed Castro Halloween Parade draw participants from all over the region.

▶ **Noe Valley:** This neighborhood was named for the original land owner, Jose de Jesus Noe who served as San Francisco's last alcalde, or mayor, during the Mexican era. Noe began his term as mayor in 1846, only to have his position stripped from him when the United States government took control after the Gold Rush. Noe Valley today is home to urban professionals and features many Victorian homes. Upscale shops like the Twenty-Fourth Street Cheese Shop now serve the locals.

▲ **Vermont Street:**

The true "crookedest" street in San Francisco, Vermont Street offers more perilous curves than Lombard Street. Sometimes termed the "blue collar Lombard Street" Vermont is not far from San Francisco General Hospital and may just be the unsung crookedest street in the whole United States.

◀ **Portrero Hill:**

Often in brilliant sunshine while other parts of the city remain covered in fog, Portrero Hill served as a cow pasture until Gold Rush squatters began displacing the cattle. From the 1860s through the twentieth century, the area primarily employed shipwrights and factory workers.

▲ **Alemany Farmer's Market:** *Opened on August 12, 1943, as an ad hoc wartime measure to conserve crops and stretch rations, the city formally assumed responsibility for managing the event in 1944. After a* *long political battle, the city used eminent domain to secure a permanent location for the market by about 1950. The farmer's market has been held here ever since and is now a favorite tradition.*

Heart of the City

In the middle of the peninsula, San Francisco sparkles with memorable gems. Made up of several small neighborhoods, each with a completely different community, Midtown San Francisco binds the city together.

Market Street passes right through the center of the Civic Center, which contains San Francisco's City Hall, the San Francisco Opera House, and several theaters and music venues. While this area contains some of the cultural highlights of the city and Union Square (as well as some of the finest shops in town), Civic Center and the nearby Tenderloin district give San Francisco that dirty urban feel. The Tenderloin, particularly, has long been known as San Francisco's worst neighborhood, one where local police earned the highest wage in the city, affording them finer cuts of meat or "tenderloin."

Nearby residential neighborhoods, Hayes Valley, Haight-Ashbury, and Cole Valley contrast with the urban inner city and display block after block of beautiful Victorian architecture. Haight-Ashbury, of course, was the birthplace of the Summer of Love in 1967, and was once home to the Grateful Dead and thousands of hippies. Today "the Haight," as locals refer to it, has given over to a lively tourist trade and sports a thriving avenue of shops, cafés, and bookstores. These western residential neighborhoods abut Golden Gate Park on the west and the Golden Gate Panhandle—an extension of the park—passes through them.

Another ethnic group makes a home here: Japantown inhabits a small area northwest of City Hall and is full of Japanese charm, culture, and architecture. Further down Market Street from the rough-edged Civic Center is an up-and-coming area sometimes called Deco Ghetto because of a small cluster of Art Deco furniture shops there. The Ghetto offers shopping, eateries, and a few music venues mostly frequented by locals.

▶ **Orpheum Theatre:** *The 2,200 seat venue opened on Market Street as the Pantages Theatre in 1926. Originally an ornate home for vaudeville entertainers, when tastes turned toward cinema in the 1930s, so did the Orpheum. The theater is now home to the Best of Broadway theatrical productions.*

◀ **City Hall:** *Rebuilt in 1915 after the building was destroyed in the 1906 earthquake, City Hall's new dome was modeled after the dome of the Church of Les Invalides in Paris. Following the Loma Prieta earthquake in 1989, restoration efforts added theatrical lighting.*

▶ **The War Memorial Opera House:** *Opening with a grand performance of Tosca in October of 1932, this building was designed by Arthur Brown, Jr., the architect who also created Coit Tower and City Hall.*

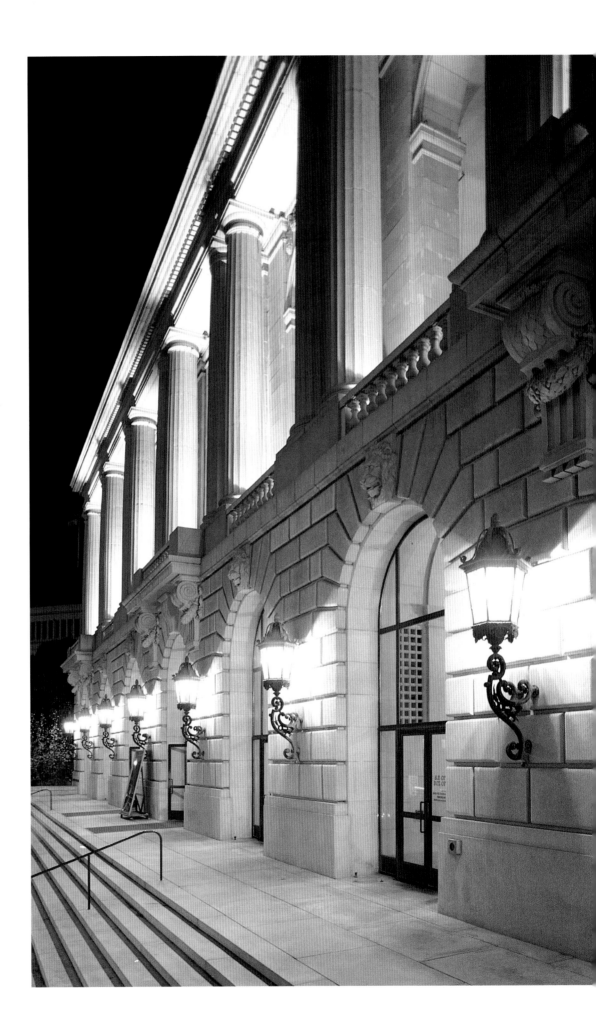

▲ **Peace Pagoda:** *A little slice of Japan, the five-tiered pagoda is the focal point of Japantown, an area to where many Japanese-American citizens returned after forced* *stays in World War II internment camps. This beautiful structure was designed by Japanese architect Yoshiro Taniguchi and opened in 1968.*

▶ **Glide Memorial United Methodist Church:** *Presided over by the Reverend Cecil Williams, who continues a ministry that he started here in 1963, this* *praiseworthy Tenderloin District church is a model of charity, serving over one million free meals a year to San Francisco's poor and needy.*

◀ **Haight Street:**
Psychedelia still reigns on the Haight, though many of the hippie shops of the 1960s have gone. Four decades after the Summer of Love, they have been replaced by eclectic boutiques and ethnic restaurants, which still recall the neighborhood's Bohemian ideals and atmosphere.

▶ **710 Ashbury Street:** *This three-story Victorian house at 710 Ashbury Street was once home to San Francisco's psychedelic band the Grateful Dead. Perhaps proving that the spirit of peace and love has not died, the house continues to draw flocks of hippie pilgrims.*

◄ **Painted Ladies:**
Perhaps the most
photographed houses in San
Francisco are the Painted
Ladies, six Queen Anne-style
homes huddled on Steiner
Street off Alamo Square.

▲ **Haight Street:**
Elaborately detailed
nineteenth-century houses
became a haven for hippies
during the 1960s. The
availability of cheap Victorian
properties for rent
encouraged the bohemian
subculture that flourished in
Haight-Ashbury.

► **San Francisco Zen
Center:** Followers of Suzuki
Roshi's teachings meditate in
a building designed in 1922
by Julia Morgan. This building
once housed the Emmanuel
Sisters, an organization that
provided a place for unwed
Jewish mothers to stay.

▲ **Union Square:**
Shoppers and tourists streak by Union Square aboard a Powell Street cable car. The city's retail and cultural center, the square was named during the Civil War for the many rallies held there in support of Union cause and troops.

▷ **Union Square, Neiman-Marcus:** *One of Union Square's upscale retail outlets is framed by palm trees in a southern view from the square. Macy's, Saks Fifth Avenue, and Levi's also hold prominent retail locations on Union Square.*

◀ **Deco Ghetto:**
Informally known as the "Deco Ghetto," a grouping of boutiques and furniture stores specializing in Art Deco are giving new identity to an area on Market Street just south-west of the Civic Center area.

▶ **Empire Plush Room:** *Once a 1920s-era speakeasy, the Empire Plush Room in the York Hotel is a key part of San Francisco's cabaret and jazz scene. Seating fewer than 120 people under a Tiffany ceiling, the club continues to lure music buffs, who no longer have to enter secretly from underground entrances.*

◀ **Boom Boom Room:**
John Lee Hooker's club opened up in the Fillmore district in 1997. Across the street from the venerable Fillmore Auditorium, the clubs here are fueling a renaissance for the area's musical heritage, once home to San Francisco's jazz scene.

Outer Neighborhoods

Out beyond Twin Peaks, San Francisco takes on a more rural, suburban feel as vast parks mingle with neighborhoods. Just south of the Presidio, the exclusive Sea Cliff mansions cling to the edge of the peninsula. What early residents referred to as the "Great Sand Waste" is now the Richmond District, a vast residential neighborhood stretching the length of Golden Gate Park. This district received a huge immigration wave from Russia and Asia after the World Wars, but the longest standing and largest population segment is Chinese. Indeed, Inner Richmond once housed the municipal and Chinese cemeteries near Lone Mountain. Now that the cemeteries have been moved out of town, Inner Richmond has garnered the nickname "Little Chinatown."

South of Golden Gate Park sits the inappropriately named Sunset District, located right in the middle of the Pacific fog belt. The microclimate around Inner Sunset is overcast more days of the year than any other part of the city. Despite the chill, many upscale residents have moved in and made the once low-priced suburb into ideal living with convenient shops, jobs, and entertainment venues. Both the Sunset and Richmond districts have a multicultural population and convenient transit options into the denser city to the east. To the west, they front on Ocean Beach, the western edge of the peninsula, and the continent.

South of the Sunset District are several small residential neighborhoods. Lakeshore, West Portal, Balboa Terrace, and Sherwood Forest combined were once the private grounds of Adolph Sutro, a San Francisco resident who made a fortune from the Comstock Lode silver miners. Sutro bought an old rancho comprising the southwestern quadrant of the city and for the most part used it to plant a forest.

▶ **Palace of the Legion of Honor:** *Commemorating the California soldiers who lost their lives in World War I, the Beaux Arts building in Lincoln Park overlooks the Pacific Ocean and houses a museum of fine arts with over 4,000 pieces in its collection, including Rodin's* The Thinker.

◀ **Lincoln Park:** *Home to the Palace of the Legion of Honor since 1923 and a community golf course since 1914, the park overlooks the Pacific and the Golden Gate Bridge. The Lincoln Highway, the country's oldest transcontinental artery, connects Lincoln Park with New York City's Times Square.*

▲ **Clement Street:** *Located in Inner Richmond, this street gives the area the name "Little Chinatown." San Francisco is home to the largest Chinese population in the United States, and a large, often overlooked portion resides here in the Richmond. Strolling down Clement Street, one can find many shops offering Chinese herbs, food, and goods.*

▶ **Richmond District:** *Looking over Golden Gate Park northeast to Inner Richmond from the De Young Museum, one can see the sprawling residential character of the Richmond District. The district's main shopping street, Clement Street, offers diverse restaurants serving food from the Far East.*

◀ **Twin Peaks:** *The Twin Peaks Tunnel opened in February 1918 to the delight of real estate developers and residents looking to move into the San Francisco "hinterlands" just west of the peaks. The two mile tunnel is the longest subway tunnel in the world and provides access to the Market Street Subway, today commonly called the Metro.*

▲ **Twin Peaks, View:** *Rising from San Francisco's center, the Twin Peaks provide some of the greatest views of the city from their 920 feet (when not shrouded in fog). Residents on the slopes of these hills live in an almost rural setting, with less traffic and bustle, but are still only a short ride from Downtown.*

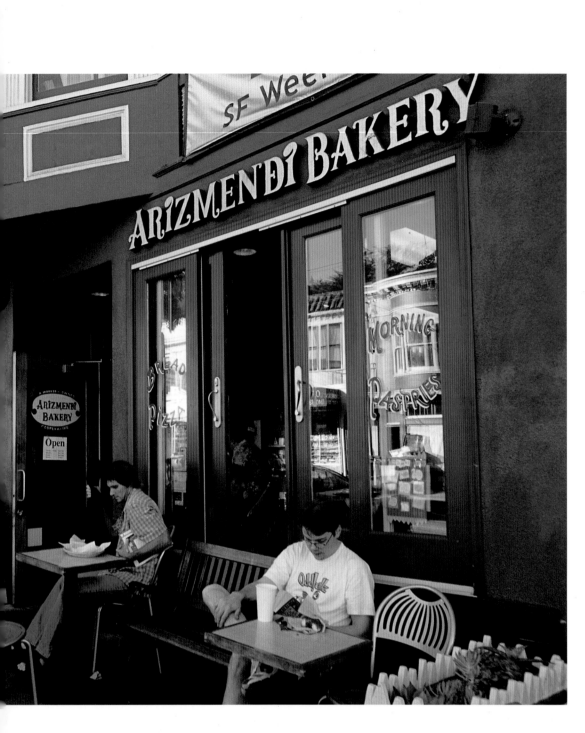

▲ **The Inner Sunset:**
*This neighborhood has
undergone gentrification in
the past twenty years or so.
Once a low-rent suburb—
noted for near constant
fog—it received an influx of
dot-com yuppies in the
1990s, raising land values
and creating a market for
upscale shops and eateries
such as this, the Arizmendi
Bakery Cooperative.*

▶ **St. Ignatius
Catholic Church:** *The
fifth church in the city, St.
Ignatius was dedicated in
1914 and overlooks the
Richmond District and the
Holy Virgin Russian Orthodox
Cathedral. The Richmond
District embraced several
waves of Russian immigrants
after the World Wars and the
Bolshevik Revolution.*

▲▲ **San Francisco National Cemetery:** Located in the Presidio, this is the final resting place for 30,000 people. Among them are 450 Buffalo Soldiers, an all African-American regiment established by Congress in 1866 to patrol America's western frontier.

▲ **Montgomery Street Barracks:** *Lining the western edge of the Presidio Parade Grounds since 1896, these five brick barracks were converted to offices by the Presidio Trust once the army deactivated the Presidio in 1994.*

▶ **Letterman Digital Arts Center:** *In 2005, filmmaker George Lucas opened this center on the site of a vacant army hospital in the historic Presidio. Famed Jedi master Yoda keeps watch from a campus fountain. The LDAC* takes its name from its location on the former site of Letterman General Hospital, which was named after Dr. Jonathan Letterman, medical director for the Army of the Potomac in the U.S. Civil War.

▶ **Cliff House:** *A Cliff House has been perched on Point Lobos since the 1860s. The first three burnt down, but the current house has survived since 1909. Restored in 2004, it is now preserved as part of the Golden Gate National Recreation Area.*

◀ **Golden Gate Park, De Young Museum:** *Founded in 1895, the De Young Museum commemorated the California Midwinter International Exposition—the West Coast's first World's Fair and the brainchild of San Francisco* Chronicle *publisher M.H. de Young. For so long a popular city museum, with a Sunday attendance of 6,000 not unusual, the museum opened in a new facility in October 2005.*

▲ **Golden Gate Park, Bison:** *In an effort to save the American bison, San Francisco began a captive breeding program in Golden Gate Park in 1891. The herd began with one pair and by 1918 had grown to thirty animals. The current herd numbers twelve. At their lowest point in 1889, only 1,100 bison were alive in the United States. Thankfully the efforts of conservationists have paid off, and today there are more than 200,000 bison.*

◀ **Golden Gate Park, Japanese Tea Garden:** *Developed as part of the California Midwinter International Exposition in 1894, the Japanese Tea Garden is thought to be the oldest public Japanese garden in the United States. Makoto Hagiwara, a wealthy landscape architect, and his family, lived in and worked on the garden from 1895 until World War II when the family was forced into a Japanese internment camp.*

▶ **Golden Gate Park, Conservatory of Flowers:** *Built in 1879, this is the oldest standing public conservatory in North America, and the anchor at the eastern end of Golden Gate Park. A pet project of San José businessman James Lick, the yet-to-be-assembled conservatory sat in crates after Lick passed away in 1876, until a group of prominent businessmen purchased it and donated it to the park commissioner the following year.*

▶ **Golden Gate Park, National AIDS Memorial Grove:** *The first of its kind in the United States, the 7.5-acre grove is located in the historic deLaveaga Dell. Founded in 1988 by a small group of San Franciscans, it is intended to provide a living tribute to those whose lives have been lost to, or touched by, AIDS. By 2003, 1,339 names were engraved here.*

▲ **Dutch Windmill:**

Sitting just inside the graffiti-covered Ocean Beach seawall, the windmill was cosmetically restored in 1980, a fitting tribute for a building that once helped transform San Francisco's western sand dunes into the lush greenbelt of Golden Gate Park.

▶ **San Francisco Zoo:**

The zoo's founder, Herbert Fleishhacker, started life as a banker, but after serving as president of the park commission, insisted San Francisco have a zoo—a proper one, with elephants! (He donated the first three: Babe, Virginia, and Marjorie.) He was successful in securing the current site for the zoo in the southwestern corner of the city, next to the largest public swimming pool in the United States, at the time, the Fleishhacker Pool. Now his dream is a reality: the zoo is home for 250 species over three acres.

Index

710 Ashbury Street 97

A

Albro, Maxine 51
Alamo Square 100
Alcatraz 14–15, 37
Alemany Farmer's Market 89
Angel Island 6, 14–15
Alioto's 28
Anza, Juan Bautista de 6–7
Arizmendi Bakery Cooperative 114
Armstrong, Lance 31
Ashbury Street 97
AT&T Park 16, 20
Ayala, Juan Manuel de 6

B

Baclutha 36–7
Balboa Terrace 106
Bank of America 6
Barbary Coast 52–3
Bartlett, Washington 9
Beaux Arts building 107
Bernal Heights 74
Bernal, Jose Cornelio de 74
Big Al's 52–3
Bimbo's 365 56
bison 121
Bliss, D. 65
Bonds, Barry 21, 31
Boom Boom Room 104
Botta, Mario 76
Broadway 53
Broadway and Columbus Mural
    56–7
Brown Jr., Arthur 93
Brown, Willie 12
Bruggen, Coosje van 23
Bush Street 58

C

Cable Car Museum 49
cable cars 14, 48, 68, 73, 102
California Palace of the Legion of
    Honor 12
California Street 10, 48, 68
Candlestick Park 12, 19, 20
Canyon of Sorrows 7
Cartoon Art Museum 81
Castro 74, 86
Castro Halloween Parade 86
Castro Street Fair 86
Chinatown 10, 11, 46, 58–9
Chinatown Gate 58–9

City Hall 12, 76, 90, 92, 93
City Lights Bookstore 12–13, 46
Civic Center 90
Clay Street 10
Clement Street 110
Cliff House 15, 118–19
Coit, Hitchcock 50
Coit Tower 46, 50–1, 93
Cole Valley 90
Columbus Street 56, 57
Condor 52–3
Conservatory of Flowers 123
Coppola, Francis Ford 63
Crabtree, Lotta 65
Crissy Field 6, 42–3
Crocker, Charles 11
"Cupid's Span" 22

D

De Young Museum 12, 120–1
Dean, Mallette Harold 51
Deco Ghetto 90, 104
Dick Hotaling's Whiskey Warehouse
    53
Divisadero Street 11
Dolores Park 84–5
Downtown 10, 11, 25, 46, 86
Dragon Lights 58
Dutch Windmill 124

E

East Bay 23
Embarcadero 8–9, 16, 24–5, 78
Embarcadero Freeway 12, 16, 25, 78
Empire Plush Room 105

F

Fair, James 66, 70
Fair, Tessie 70
Fairmont Hotel 70–1
Faville, William B. 65
ferries 37
Ferry Building 8–9, 12, 16, 16–17, 22,
    25, 76
Ferry Building farmer's market 25
Filbert Street 53
Financial District 46
Fisherman's Wharf 16, 28–9, 33
Fleishhacker, Herbert 124
Fleishhacker Pool 124
Flood Building 67
Flood, James 11, 66, 70
Flood Mansion 70
Font, Pedro 7

Fog City Diner 26
Forest Hill 11
Fort Mason 6
Fort Point 40
Franklin Street 73

G

Gandhi Statue 25
Geary Theater 64
Ghirardelli Square 34, 35
Giannini, Steve 51
Gilde Memorial United Methodist
    Church 95
Giuntoli, Agostino 56
Goddess of Democracy (statue) 60
Golden Gate Bridge 16, 38–9, 108–9
Golden Gate National Recreation
    Area 118
Golden Gate Panhandle 90
Golden Gate Park 90, 106, 121, 122,
    123
Gough, Charles H. 9
Gough, Octavia 9
Grace Cathedral 46, 68, 69
Grant Avenue 10, 11, 53, 58
Grant Street 46
Grateful Dead 90, 96

H

Haas-Lilienthal House 72
Haas, William 73
Hagiwara, Makoto 122
Haight-Ashbury 90, 100
Haight Street 96, 100
Hallidie, Andrew 10, 49
Hammett, Dashiell 66
Hang Ah Restaurant 58
Haro, Don Francisco de 83
Hayes Valley 90
Hearst, William Randolph 63
Holy Virgin Russian Orthodox
    Church 115
Hooker, John Lee 104
Hopkins, Mark 11
Hungry I Club 52–3
Huntingdon, Collis P. 11, 46
Huntingdon Hotel 47
Hyde Street 14–15, 73
Hyde Street Pier 15
Hyde Street Cable Car 14–15

I

Inner Richmond 106, 110
Inner Sunset 106, 114

J
Jackson Street 53
Japanese Tea Garden *122*
Japantown 90, 94
Jeremiah O'Brien (troop ship) *33*
John's Grill *66*

K
Kearny Street 11
Klaas, Tony 57

L
Lakeshore 106
Lee, Noel 18
Letterman Digital Arts Center *117*
Lick, James 123
Lincoln Avenue 11
Lincoln Highway 110
Lincoln Park 106, *108–9*
"Little Chinatown" 106, *110*
Loma Prieta Earthquake 12, 16, 93
Lombard Street 46, *73*, 88
Lone Mountain 106
Lotta's Fountain *65*
Lucas, George 116

M
Mackay, John 66
Marina District 12
Market Street 10, 15, 46, 63, 74, *76*,
    78, 90
Marsh, Thomas 61
Marshall, James W. 9
Maybeck, Bernard 45
McCovey Cove *21*
McCovey, Willie 21
Metreon 74, *75*
Midtown 90–105
Milk, Harvey 86
Mission District 74, *83*
Mission Dolores 46, 74, 83
Mission Dolores Basilica 7
Mission San Francisco De Asis 7, 7–8,
    82
Mission Street 9, 74, *82*
Monster Park *18–19, 20*
Montgomery, J. B. 9
Montgomery Street Barracks *116*
Morgan, Julia 63, 70, 100
Moscone Convention Center 74
Mount Tamalpais 35, *37*
Musée Mécanique *32*

N
National AIDS Memorial Grove *123*
Neiman-Marcus *102–3*
Nob Hill 10–11, 46
Nob Hill Spa *47*
Noe, Jose de Jesus 9, 86
Noe Valley 9, 74, *86–7*
North Beach 46, 53
North of Market 46–73

O
Oakland Athletics 12
O'Brien, William 66
Ocean Beach 11, *15*, 106, 124
O'Farrell, Jaspar 9
Old United States Mint 74, *80–1*
Oldenburg, Claes 23
Orpheum Theatre *91*
Ortega, Jose Francisco de 6
O'Shaughnessy Seawall 11

P
Pac Bell Park 21
Pacific Heights 9, 46
Pacific Street 53
Pacific Union Club *70*
Painted Ladies *98–9*
Palace of Fine Arts *44–5*
Palace of the Legion of Honor *107*,
    110
Pampanito, USS *33*
Panama Pacific International
    Exposition 42, 45
Peace Pagoda *94*
Pier 39 16, *27*
Pissis, Albert 66
Point Lobos *118 19*
Polk, Willis 70
Portola, Don Gaspar de 6
Portsmouth Square 10
Potrero Hill 73, 74, *88*
Powell Street 1, 102
Presidio 46, 106, 116

R
Richardson, William 8–9
Richmond District 106, *110–11*, 114
Ruef, Abe 63
Russian Hill 46

S
Sacramento Street 9
St. Francis Wood 11
St. Francis Yacht Club *45*
St. Ignatius Catholic Church *114–15*
Saints Peter and Paul Church *54–5*
San Francisco Bay 28, 45
San Francisco Drydock 23
San Francisco 49ers 19
San Francisco Giants 12, 16, 20, 21
San Francisco Museum of Modern
    Art 12, 74, *76–7*
San Francisco National Cemetery
    116
San Francisco-Oakland Bay Bridge
    40–1, 48
San Francisco Port 23
San Francisco Zen Center *100–1*
San Francisco Zoo *124–5*
San Mateo County 15
San Miguel rancho 9
Sausalito 35

Schmidt, Peter 73
Schulz, Charles M. 81
Sea Cliff 106
Sentinal Building
Sherwood Forest 106
Sloat Boulevard 11
South of Market 12, 74–89
SouthWest Marine 23
Stanford, Leland 11
Steiner, L. 9
Steiner Street 100
Stinking Rose, The *57*
Stone's Boat Yard 45
Strauss, Joseph Baerman 40
Streetcars *78–9*
Sunset District 11, 106
Sutro, Adolph 106
Sutro Baths 6
Sydney Town 53

T
Tadich Grill *61*
Taniguchi, Yoshiro 94
Telegraph Hill 46, 50, 53
Tenderloin District 90, 94
Third Street 63
Thirtieth Street 11
Transamerica Pyramid 6
Treasure Island *23*
Twin Peaks 74, *112, 113*
Twin Peaks Tunnel 11, 113

U
Union Iron Works *23*
Union Square 90, *102–3*
Union Street 46

V
Van Ness, James 10
Vancouver, Richard 8
Vermont Street 73, *88*
Vioget, J. J. 9

W
Waterfront 16–45
War Memorial Opera House 90, *93*
Wax Museum *30, 31*
Weber, Bill 57
West Portal 11, 106
Westwood Park 11
Williams, Cecil 94

Y
Yelamu people 6
Yerba Buena 9
Yerba Buena Gardens 12, 74, 81
Yerba Buena Island 40
York Hotel 104
Young, M. H. de 121
Young, Monk 56

Map of San Francisco

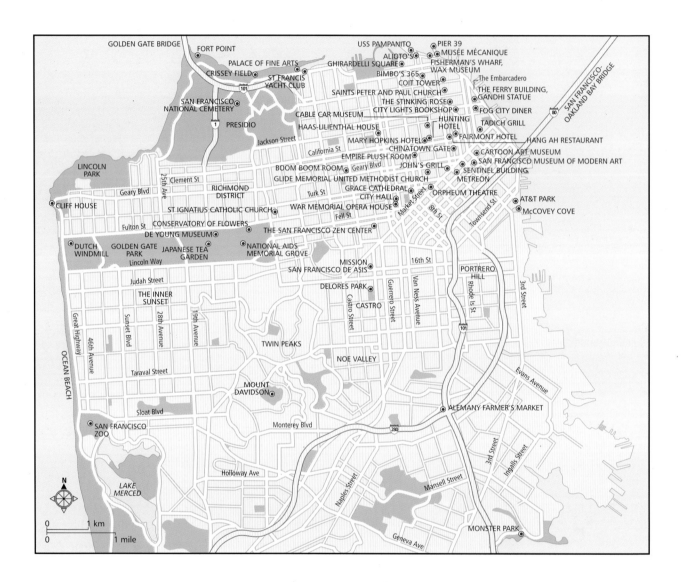

GOLDEN GATE BRIDGE
FORT POINT
USS PAMPANITO
PIER 39
MUSÉE MÉCANIQUE
ALIOTO'S
PALACE OF FINE ARTS
GHIRARDELLI SQUARE
FISHERMAN'S WHARF,
WAX MUSEUM
CRISSEY FIELD
BIMBO'S 365
ST FRANCIS
YACHT CLUB
COIT TOWER
The Embarcadero
SAINTS PETER AND PAUL CHURCH
THE FERRY BUILDING,
GANDHI STATUE
SAN FRANCISCO
NATIONAL CEMETERY
THE STINKING ROSE
CITY LIGHTS BOOKSHOP
FOG CITY DINER
CABLE CAR MUSEUM
HUNTING
HOTEL
TADICH GRILL
PRESIDIO
HAAS-LILIENTHAL HOUSE
MARY HOPKINS HOTEL
FAIRMONT HOTEL
HANG AH RESTAURANT
Jackson Street
CHINATOWN GATE
California St
EMPIRE PLUSH ROOM
CARTOON ART MUSEUM
LINCOLN
PARK
BOOM BOOM ROOM
Geary Blvd
JOHN'S GRILL
SAN FRANCISCO MUSEUM OF MODERN ART
25th Ave
Clement St
GLIDE MEMORIAL UNITED METHODIST CHURCH
SENTINEL BUILDING
METREON
Geary Blvd
RICHMOND
DISTRICT
GRACE CATHEDRAL
ORPHEUM THEATRE
Turk St
CITY HALL
AT&T PARK
CLIFF HOUSE
ST IGNATIUS CATHOLIC CHURCH
WAR MEMORIAL OPERA HOUSE
McCOVEY COVE
Fell St
Townsend St
Fulton St
CONSERVATORY OF FLOWERS
THE SAN FRANCISCO ZEN CENTER
DE YOUNG MUSEUM
DUTCH
WINDMILL
GOLDEN GATE
PARK
JAPANESE TEA
GARDEN
NATIONAL AIDS
MEMORIAL GROVE
Lincoln Way
MISSION
16th St
PORTRERO
HILL
Judah Street
SAN FRANCISCO DE ASIS
THE INNER
SUNSET
DELORES PARK
28th Avenue
19th Avenue
Castro Street
CASTRO
Guerrero Street
Van Ness Avenue
Rhode Is St
3rd Street
Sunset Blvd
46th Avenue
TWIN PEAKS
NOE VALLEY
Taraval Street
MOUNT
DAVIDSON
Evans Avenue
Sloat Blvd
ALEMANY FARMER'S MARKET
SAN FRANCISCO
ZOO
Monterey Blvd
3rd Street
Ingalls Street
Holloway Ave
Mansell Street
LAKE
MERCED
Naples Street
MONSTER PARK
Geneva Ave

N

0   1 km
0   1 mile